LIFE OF
PAT F. GARRETT
AND THE TAMING OF THE BORDER OUTLAW.

A HISTORY OF THE "GUN MEN" AND OUTLAWS, AND A LIFE-STORY OF THE GREATEST SHERIFF OF THE OLD SOUTHWEST.

BY JOHN MILTON SCANLAND

PUBLISHED BY
CARLETON F. HODGE
EL PASO, TEXAS.

FILTER PRESS
Palmer Lake, Colorado 80133
1971

IN MEMORY OF JOHN J. LIPSEY

HE KILLED BILLY THE KID!

This is a facsimile reprint of one of the most sought-for items of New Mexicana, a famous but almost never seen booklet about the sheriff who pursued and killed Billy the Kid. It was written just after Garrett's own slaying in 1908, written by a newspaperman who knew Garrett and New Mexico well. This exact reproduction was made by a photographic process from one of the two known copies of the first (and until now only) edition. It is not only good history; it is thrilling reading matter. No collection of Western Outlaw material is complete without it.

John J. Lipsey, Western Historian, Rare-book dealer, author, and publisher, wrote the above paragraph when he first reprinted this book in 1952. Shortly after John died in 1969, Julia asked if I wouldn't like to reprint the book again. I am fortunate, and proud to be able to bring it to a new generation of Americana collectors, using John's printing plates.

G.L. Campbell January 1971

SBN 910584-18-4

THE FILTER PRESS
P.O. BOX 5
PALMER LAKE, COLORADO 80133

Pat. F. Garrett

¶

CHAPTER I

"Pat" F. Garrett, the slayer of "Billy, the Kid," was killed by Wayne Brazel, near Las Cruces, New Mexico, on the morning of February 29, 1908. The weapon used was a six-shooter and the first shot entered the back of the head and came out over the left eye; the second ball entered the lower breast and ranged up about nine inches into the shoulder blade. Garrett died instantly, and without speaking.

The tragedy occurred five miles east of the village. Garrett was in his buggy, with Carl Adamson, and Brazel was on horseback, having overtaken Garrett, who was on his way to Las Cruces. Brazel rode on to town and surrendered to Sheriff Lucero, stating that he had killed Garrett in self-defense. Brazel was placed in jail, and a coroner's jury was impanelled, and went to the scene of the killing. The jury gave a formal verdict merely stating that the deceased came to his death at the hands of Wayne Brazel. On the following Monday, two days afterwards, Dudley Poe Garrett, son of the deceased, officially charged Brazel with the murder.

"Pat" Garrett, the famous hunter of desperadoes, was buried in the little graveyard at Las Cruces (The Crosses) on the following Thursday. The cortege was covered with fioral offerings, and followed to the grave by his many friends. The funeral was delayed at the request of his brothers, John and A. J. Garrett, of Haynesville, Louisiana, who desired to attend. The pall-bearers were: Hon. George Curry, Governor of New Mexico; Harry Lane, Morgan Llewellyn, Numa G. Buchoz and Thomas Powers. Not being a member of any religious denomination, it was understood as Garrett's desire, that no minister should officiate at his funeral. Accordingly, he was buried without this ceremony, the only burial rites being the reading of an oration by Thomas Powers, of El Paso, which was written by Robert Ingersoll, and read at the grave of his brother.

"Dear Friends:

"We have assembled here to pay a last tribute to the love and loving brother, husband, father, friend, who died wher manhood's morning almost touches noon, and while the shad ows still were falling toward the west.

"He had not passed on life's highway the stone that mark the highest point, while yet in love with life and enrapture with the world, he passed to silence and pathetic dust.

"Yet, after all, it may be best, just in the happiest, sunni est hour of all the voyage, while eager winds are kissing ever sail, to dash against the unseen rock, and in an instant hea the billows roar above a sunken ship. For whether in mi sea or 'mong the breakers of the farther shore, a wreck at las must mark the end of each and all. And every life, no matte if its every hour is rich with love and every moment jewelle with a joy, will, at its close, become a tragedy as sad and dee and dark as can be woven of the warp and woof of mystery an death.

TOM POWERS.

"This brave and tender man in every storm of life was oak and rock; but in sunshine he was vine and flower. He was the friend of all herioc souls. He climbed the heights, and left all superstitions far below, while on his forehead fell the golden dawning of a grander day.

"He loved the beautiful, and was with color, form and music touched to tears. He sided with the weak, the poor, and wronged, and lovingly gave alms. With loyal heart and with the purest hands he faithfully discharged all public trusts.

"He was a worshiper of liberty, a friend of the oppressed. He believed that happiness is the only good, reason the only touch, justice the only worship, humanity the only religion, and love the only priest. He added to the sum of human joy; and were every one to whom he did some loving service bring a blossom to his grave, he would sleep tonight beneath a wilderness of flowers.

"Life is a narrow vale between the cold and barren peaks of two eternities. We strive in vain to look beyond the heights. We cry aloud, and the only answer is the echo of our wailing cry. From the voiceless lips of the unreplying dead there comes no word; but in the night of death hope sees a star and listening love can hear the rustle of a wing.

"The record of a generous life runs like a vine around the memory of our dead, and every sweet, unselfish act is now a perfumed flower.

"And now, to you, who have been chosen from among the many men he loved, to do the last sad office for the dead, we give his sacred dust.

"Speech cannot contain our love. There was, there is, no gentler, stronger, manlier man."

Though simple and not attended by ostentation, the ceremonial was very impressive, and there were tears for the brave and generous "Pat" Garrett as his mortal remains were consigned to earth.

CHAPTER II.

ORIGIN OF THE TROUBLE.

Neighborhood quarrels, like wars between nations, are mostly caused by boundary disputes, or trespassing. This tragedy grew out of a misunderstanding as to whether goats or cattle should graze upon a ranch which Brazel had leased from Garrett. Pat Garrett owned two ranches in the Organ mountains, about 25 miles east of Las Cruces, upon one of which he had been living about two years, or since the expiration of his term of office as Collector of Customs at El Paso Texas. It seems that he owed about $3,000 to a merchant in Las Cruces, and to secure the debt, he gave a mortgage. The merchant agreeing to take $2,000 for the debt, Garrett borrowed that sum from W. W. Cox, of the San Augustine ranch near by, giving him a mortgage on the ranch and stock. The matter was further complicated in Cox negligently permitting the mortgage to lapse, and a bank, which had a judgment against Garrett, seized and sold Garrett's stock under attachment. But the sheriff did not find all of the stock, a part being in Cox's pasture, which Cox then attached. Cox then conveyed the stock back to Garrett, but as Garrett did not have enough stock for his Bear Canyon ranch, he leased it to Wayne Brazel and A. P. Rhodes, the latter being related to Cox.

Unfortunately, and to still further complicate matters, the written contract did not specify the kind of stock to be kept on the ranch, but Garrett said that Brazel verbally promised to keep 300 to 400 head of cattle, while Brazel states that nothing was said regarding the stock and that he (Brazel) intended to keep goats on the ranch and as soon as he took possession of the ranch he stocked it with goats.

This angered Garrett because he realized that the goats would soon ruin the range for cattle and horses and he now desired to get Brazel and Rhodes off the ranch.

In January Garrett had Brazel arrested under an old statue in New Mexico making it a misdemeanor to herd stock within a mile and a half of a ranch house or settlement, but the justice of the peace dismissed the case and Garrett realized that his only course was to buy Brazel out, or transfer the lease.

THE QUESTION OF SHEEP, GOATS OR CATTLE.

A few weeks before the tragedy J. P. Miller, of Fort

Worth, Texas, and Carl Adamson, of Roswell, New Mexico, approached Pat Garrett with an offer to buy his ranch. Miller and Garrett had known each other for several years, Miller being marshal in Pecos City when Garrett was sheriff of Lincoln county. Garrett and Adamson had never met before. In the beginning of the proposed deal, Garrett stated he "would have to get a goat man off, first," referring to Brazel, and the lease. Garrett arranged a meeting between Miller and Brazel. and Brazel agreed to sell his goats at $3.50 each, and surrender the lease. In the contract Brazel stated that he had 1200 goats. A few days later he reported that he had 1800. This was the turning point in the transaction, or rather, which caused the deal to fail, and led to the shooting, according to the statements of Adamson. Miller and Adamson did not particularly want the goats, but consented to buy 1200 in order to get the lease. But they refused to take 1800, and Brazel refused to surrender the lease if they did not. It was at this point that Garrett sought for legal advice in El Paso a few days before his death, his aim being to oust Brazel by legal proceedings. The stipulated price for the ranch was $3,000.

CHAPTER III.

THE TRAGEDY ON THE LONELY ROAD.

On the day before the tragedy, Carl Adamson hired a team and buggy and went to Garrett's ranch to bring him on the next day to Las Cruces; also, to notify Brazel to meet Garrett there, so as to arrange terms for the ranch. Adamson remained that night at Garrett's. Next morning they started for Las Cruces in the buggy. Garrett placed in the buggy his Burgess, or "folding" rifle, which could be folded and carried in a holster, like a revolver, being snapped together in gun form when pulled from the holster. In placing it in the buggy Garrett remarked, according to the statement of Adamson. "I'll place this between us, because we may have trouble before we get to town." The gun was loaded with six shells of No. 8 bird shot. They overtook Brazel just beyond the settlement of Organ. He had a Winchester rifle strapped to his saddle; also, a revolver on his left side. Brazel rode along by the buggy, keeping his right side toward the buggy. Consequently, Garrett did not know that he also carried a revolver, but kept his eye on the Winchester. The terms of the lease were discussed.

and as the discussion grew warm, Adamson said he stopped the buggy to arrange the harness. He did not state whether it was merely disarranged, or broken. His statement is as follows:

CARL ADAMSON'S STATEMENT.

Adamson stated in an interview that he got out of the buggy to fix the harness, and that while standing beside the buggy, he heard Garrett say to Brazel, "I don't give a ——— whether you sell all your goats and give up the lease, or not. I can get you off any way; I'll put you out right now." Garrett then leaped from the buggy, Adamson says, "but I don't know whether he grabbed his gun as he did so, or whether he got his gun later—after Brazel had shot him and before he fell. I did not see as I was on the other side of the horse. I know that when Garrett fell he dropped his gun, and it had not been fired. It was a folding pump gun, and loaded with bird shot. I am sure that Garrett did not know that Brazel had a revolver. He saw Brazel's Winchester strapped beside him on the horse, and had his eye on that. I am sure he thought he could cover Brazel with his shotgun before Brazel could draw the Winchester, and so he did not count on Brazel's revolver, as he did not know that he had one. As Garrett fell to the ground he was dead. There were two bullet holes in his body; I am not positive whether the first shot hit him in the back of the head or the breast. I stepped from behind the rig just as he fell, and Brazel got off his horse and coolly said: 'This is hell!' He handed me his revolver, and got into the buggy. I put a lap robe over the corpse, and, hitching Brazel's horse behind the buggy, we drove to Las Cruces, and Brazel surrendered, saying he killed Garrett in self defense."

CHAPTER IV.

GARRETT HAD A PRESENTIMENT OF HIS FATE.

This is one of the most noted tragedies in the history of the Southwest, celebrated for its many deeds of blood. It attracted general attention throughout the west, and great excitement in Dona Ana, Lincoln and adjoining sections where Garrett was personally known. He was personally known to more men in the Southwest than any other man in the country, and was known by reputation almost throughout the entire country as the slayer of the desperado, William H. Bonney, alias "Billy the Kid." The news of his violent death was received with consternation, especially as it was known that he was ever on the alert against being surprised by the friends of outlaws whom he had brought to justice, or killed while resisting arrest. It was strange that he should be unprepared, or rather not on his guard, was the general remark, and many hinted at a plot. These hints broadened into what the friends of Garrett deemed well-grounded suspicions, when it was remembered that about a week before the tragedy, Garrett had informed Governor Curry, and other friends in El Paso, that he expected trouble from the very source whence it came. Strangely, and as if directed by Fate to his doom, he took no precautions to avoid what he saw was inevitable! There is something that guides us to our Destiny, even against our discretion and reason. And so it seems was the case of Patrick Garrett. On the morning of the day when he was to meet Brazel, his slayer, at the village of Las Cruces, to settle the matter of the lease of the ranch, which had for some time been a source of trouble, he dressed with unusual care! Was it a presentiment that he was preparing for the grave? He alone knew! His shotgun was loaded with bird shot—evidence that he did not expect to use his weapon—or, rather, it was contrary to his presentiment of impending danger. He knew, as all "gun men" know, that bird shot, even at very close range, is very seldom, if ever, instantly fatal. And, stranger still, that one with his experience, and skill with a gun, should, in a quarrel, permit his antagonist to "get the drop" on him. That he did not expect trouble at that moment is evidenced from the fact that his antagonist did "get the drop" on him, is the belief of all who knew Garrett, and his record warrants this belief. The sworn statement of Carl Adamson, the only living witness to the tragedy except Brazel, is also corroborative of this belief. This statement is that while arranging the harness Garrett got out of the buggy and that his back was partly turned from Barzel when the shot was fired. He further states that Garrett took his shotgun out of the buggy, and had threatened Brazel. Such men as Garrett do not make threats. They shoot first. Furthermore, had he made a threat, there was no use in getting out of the buggy to carry it into execution—he could have shot from where he sat. Besides, he would not have partly turned his back to his antagonist, after getting out of the buggy, with his gun, and making the threat—if such was the truth! His clothing being partly disarranged when the corpse was viewed by the conorer, shows that he got out of the buggy for another purpose; and, his back being partly turned from Brazel, is evidence that he did not expect trouble at that time, and had made no preparations for defense. That is how Brazel got the drop on him, is argued by his friends.

MYSTERY AND SUSPICION.

There is a mystery about this tragedy, and it may never come to light. Whether there was a plot is unknown; yet, suspicions are strong that there was. It is hinted by the friends of Garrett that astounding revelations will be made. The theory advanced for these revelations is that there was a plot to kill Garrett. Brazel claims that he did the shooting in self defense, that is, knowing Garrett's record as a gun fighter, he did not desire to take any chances, and shot first. In getting out of the buggy, Garrett casually remarked: "I'll get you off the ranch, anyway!" This meant, legally; though Brazel construed it as a threat, notwithstanding that Garrett made no demonstration with his gun—if he had his gun at the time, which is very doubtful. It is contrary to reason that any one should make a threat and make no preparations to defend himself, as in this case. Everything points to the contrary. What his suspicions were of impending trouble Garrett never communicated to any one—only that he expected there would be trouble, "and if he did not get them, they would get him!" This hinted at a league against him, or a plot. A few days before his violent death he visited El Paso and consulted a lawyer as to the means of cancelling the lease of his ranch to Brazel, who, he claimed, had violated that lease, and this legal method of removing him from the ranch is what Garrett meant when he got out of the buggy, during the heated controversy, and which Brazel understood, or pretended to understand, as a threat.

Brazel is a typical cowboy in appearance, and to emphasize it, wears a black broad-brimmed black hat, the crown pushed up high, and the hat pulled well over his ears. He is 31 years of age, and is unmarried. He states that he knew Garrett 20 years ago when Garrett lived in Lincoln county. He has a rudy complexion, sandy hair, rough features, is strongly built, and is smooth shaven. He has a scar reaching from the right corner of his mouth down over his chin, evidently a wound from a knife. It is not known if he has a gun record.

CHAPTER V.

AT THE BAR OF JUSTICE.

The preliminary hearing of Wayne Brazel, charged with the murder of Patrick F. Garrett, was held in the Dona Ana county court room on Wednesday afternoon following the shooting. Justice of the Peace Manuel Lopez presided. The little court room was crowded by the many friends of Garrett, including Governor Curry. At the time the corpse of Garrett was in the undertaking rooms a short distance away, and prior to the beginning of the case Governor Curry and many others viewed the remains of their departed friend. Governor Curry then called upon the bereaved widow and tendered his heartfelt sympathies to the family.

The prisoner, Wayne Brazel, was accompanied in the court room by his friend, W. W. Cox, his constant companion before the tragedy. Cox is not related to Brazel, but they had always been "close friends." Brazel occupied the prisoner's chair, facing the justice, and seemed nervous and ill at ease. The two attorneys for the defense sat at the right. Attorney General J. M. Hervey, who had charge of the prosecution, sat to the left of the prisoner. A few feet distant sat Dudley Poe Garrett and his sisters, Elizabeth and Annie.

THE TESTIMONY OF THE ONLY WITNESS.

Carl Adamson, the only witness to the tragedy, testified that he was a comparative stranger to both Brazel and Garrett, and that he had driven to Garrett's ranch to bring him to Las Cruces to there meet Brazel, and arrange the matter of the lease. They overtook Brazel just beyond Organ, and at times he rode ahead, and again behind, the conversation continuing the while about the lease, and especially about the goats. Finally, Garrett asked Brazel how it came that he (Brazel) had signed a contract for 1200 goats when he had 1800. Brazel replied that he did not think he had 1800, but that if he did not sell the whole bunch he would not sell any, and would keep possession of the ranch. "I then told Garrett that I did not want 1800 goats, and that might break up the deal. This made Garrett angry, and then Garrett said to Brazel, 'I don't care whether you give up the ranch or not; I'll get you off, anyway.' Brazel then said, 'I don't know whether you can or not!' About that time I stopped the buggy, for a certain purpose and Garrett took the lines. When I was standing by the side of the buggy, I heard Garrett say, '—— you, I'll get you off now,' or something like that. Brazel was on his horse at my back. I did not hear what else was said, but when I heard the shots I turned and saw Garrett on the ground about two feet from the buggy; Brazel was on his horse, a little in front of the buggy and even with the team. He was sitting on his horse with his six-shooter in his hand. After the first shot Garrett staggered back and fell, his shotgun was by his side; Garrett was dead when I got to him; he never spoke, but groaned a little; I put the laprobe over the corpse and came with Brazel to Las Cruces."

Brazel was admitted to $10,000 bail. There was considerable surprise and comment at the small amount. The bondsmen are: B. F. Lane, Henry Stoes, J. S. Queensberry, J. W. Taylor, Jeff Isaacs, Geo. W. Freeman, F. H. Bascom, W. W. Cox.

CHAPTER VI.

RUMORS OF THREATS.

Naturally, Garrett had enemies—all men of prominence have. There ever lurks in the by-ways of life the envious and the unsuccessful, who hurl their venom and slanders upon those who have succeeded, merely because they are successful. A man of the law is naturally hated by the lawless, and this famous hunter of desperadoes knew that he was both feared and hated by this class and their sympathizers. Several times he stated that he "expected to die with his boots on." He had heard a few weeks before his death that threats had been made against his life, but he had been threatened so often that it became an old story. However, the signs of impending trouble were so ominous that he informed Governor Curry and the threatened trouble seemed of such magnitude that the governor decided to send several rangers into the Organ mountains to preserve the peace. But, unfortunately, the trouble came sooner than expected, and from an unexpected source.

SHADOWS LURKING IN THE DARKNESS.

One night about two weeks before the tragedy the figures of two men were seen moving about Garrett's ranch house by Frank Adams, a workman on the place. He was awakened by the noise, and silently watched the two figures sneaking up to the house. He awakened Garrett, but Garrett thought the noise was made by dogs and that the man was mistaken as to seeing the figures of men. The prowlers were evidently frightened away by the conversation of Garrett and Adams. Next morning Adams investigated and found the well defined foot prints of two men near the ranch house where he thought he saw the figures stealthily moving forward, and he also found the tracks of two horses in the ravine, where they had been tethered while the men sought to creep up to the house.

A MYSTERIOUS LETTER.

Four days after the tragedy Dudley Poe Garrett, son of Pat Garrett, and who swore to the official complaint against the slayer of his father, received a note scrawled in lead pencil, warning him that he would be killed as was his father. The writer professed to be a friend of Garrett, and stated that "Brazel shot Garrett from the back and that another shot him from the front." The unknown writer, who signed himself as "One Who Knows," concluded that "Hanging without trial is what Brazel should get."

As Carl Adamson was the only witness to the tragedy, and as that fact was well known, it is very strange that any one should sign himself as "One Who Knows." This deepens the mystery surrounding the strange tragedy.

CHAPTER VII.

THE LIFE OF GARRETT.

Patrick F. Garrett was born in Chambers county, Alabama, on June 5, 1850, and was aged 57 years at the time of his death. He was of Scotch-Irish parentage. From Alabama the family went to Claiborne parish, Louisiana, and located near the village of Haynesville. When about 17 years of age he left Louisiana and went west. He lived a few years in Lancaster, Texas, and then in Uvalde county. In 1879 he was united in marriage with Miss Guitterez, who is related to the historic Spanish family of that name, one of whom was governor of California before the American conquest. By this marriage there were seven children: Dudley Poe, Elizabeth, Annie, Patrick, Pauline, Oscar and Jarvis Powers, the latter being aged three years. He was appointed deputy sheriff of Lincoln county in 1879 and in 1881 he was elected sheriff, which position he held two years. He then bought a ranch near Roswell, where he remained until 1896, when he was persuaded to accept the office of deputy sheriff in Dona Ana county and restore order in that crime-ridden section. Two years later he was elected sheriff, and at the end of his term had succeeded in restoring order as he had done in Lincoln. In 1902 he was appointed collector of customs at El Paso, Texas, which position he held four years. At the end of his term he moved back to his ranch in the Organ mountains, about 25 miles from Las Cruces.

Pat Garrett impressed one as very thoughtful and of a frank, friendly nature. He was unassuming, peaceably inclined, and was a man of few words. He always spoke to the point, and mildly. To his strong personality was due much of his success as an officer. He reasoned only with men of education and reason, and never argued with the stubborn and the ignorant. Thus, he avoided many quarrels and difficulties which men of less discernment and judge of human nature encountered. He had steel blue eyes which seemed to look through a man, and a glance told the desperado that he had a man of courage to deal with. His hair and mustache were dark, his physique was strong and firm, he was six feet and four inches in stature, and his entire personality denoted a man of the unusual type—one born to command, and who would become prominent in any age and in any country. He leaves a widow and seven children to mourn his untimely death.

CHAPTER VIII.

THE REIGN OF THE "GUN MEN."

The "Dark Ages" of southeastern New Mexico covers the period in local history from about 1878 to 1882. That is, this is the historic Dark Age. Before that time little is known, as records of crimes were imperfectly kept, or rather not kept.

Unlike the Dark Ages in mediaeval times, more of the history of this period is written than the ages preceding, contradictory as it may seem. Before this period the courts were imperfectly organized and the laws were practically a dead letter, so far as their enforcement was concerned. Several conditions united to make this particular section a land of bloody murders. As each section of the United States became settled and orderly, the "bad men" sought new and unprotected fields where they could rob and murder with little fear of punishment. Situated on the northwestern border of Texas, adjoining Arizona on the east, and Mexico on the south, that territory now known as Lincoln and Dona Ana counties received most of the overflow of "gun men," cattle rustlers, liquor traders, gamblers, bullies Mexican horse thieves, and the scum of civilization. They fled to this "pocket" on the southwestern frontier where for a time they were secluded and were not reached by the advancing wave of civilization. The geographical position of the country had much to do with its feuds and cattle wars. Penologists hold that crime is inherent, that is, a person is born with the desire to commit crime. But in this instance it is due more to geography than to inherent nature. At the several military posts were stationed from 1000 to 2000 soldiers, but their duties were to hold in check the Indians and only aided the civil authorities when called upon to suppress a riot. Most of the soldiers were disorderly, and had little taste for Indian fighting, and less for target practice with the "gun men," who came in to "shoot up" a town.

GOOD AND BAD "GUN MEN."

There were all kinds of "gun men" in this "bloody district," perhaps the bloodiest in the United States, considering its area, and small population. The genuine "bad men" did not look as if he would fight under any provocation. He was not the long-haired blusterer, like the "Captain Jacks" and the "Hanks" found in every section; nor like the braggart Earps of infamous Arizona record, who fled to California in advance of a vigilance committee. Nor did the real gun man speak the dialect attributed to him by writers of "fake" fiction in the cheap magazines of the East. He was quiet in manner, slow in speech, and respectful in tone; he was unassuming, and had no swaggering gait like the "bully." He was about the last man any one would take to be a gun man, and he was about the first one whom the swaggering bully, seeking to get up a reputation, would select as a victim. The real bad man was of course always armed, and he was quick on the draw. He made short work of the bully. And, thus, quarrels were usually forced upon him, and he killed in self defense. And, strangely, when a bad man had thus established a reputation, though forced upon him, he was compelled to fight to maintain it. There were bad men who killed for the love of killing—they were naturally depraved, murderers at heart, like "Billy the Kid." They craved the excitement of committing a murder, and gloated in the shedding of human blood, as does the brutal Mexican bullfighter in slaughtering his defenseless victim. But these real bad men never shot from ambush—they shot in the open, but generally aimed to get the "drop" on their enemies. They gave their antagonist a chance, and he usually got in a shot, and sometimes it was effective. The real gun men scorned to shoot from ambush, or in the back, like the cowardly assassins of the "Jim" Hargis and W. B. Hawkins type, who have stained the beautiful Blue Grass region of Kentucky with their inhuman crimes. Unlike these Kentucky "Night Riders," the gun men of southeastern New Mexico did not make war upon women and children—they fought men. Unlike the "Dark and Bloody Ground" of Kentucky, which had been settled for a hundred years, this section was new—only recently acquired from Mexico, and now partly occupied by Indians still uncivilized, and by Mexicans who hated the conquering "Gringo." These, with the lawless element from adjacent sections, united to make it a "storm center" of disorder. But still, it was not so bad as that section of Kentucky now terrorized by the incendiary "Night Riders." A man was given a chance, and though his antagonist had the drop on him, still it was a chance.

CHAPTER IX.

BLOODY DONA ANA COUNTY.

Dona Ana county, a section where the "cattle rustlers' war" raged with all the fierceness and brutality natural to bloodthirsty outlaws, is situated on the southwestern border, between Grant county on the west and Lincoln county on the east. It was Mexican territory and acquired by the United States in 1853, being part of the "Gadsden Purchase." It was first settled by a colony from Chihuahua in the early fifties, but when the territory was bought by the United States most of the colonists returned to Chihuahua rather than remain in the country of the hated "gringo." The United States was fortunate in getting rid of this criminal element, but others came across the border--horse thieves and bandits, and thus it was "bad lands" from the beginning. The name Dona Ana is from the wife of one of the colonists. The county seat was located first at the village of Dona Ana, then changed to Las Cruces, then to Mesilla, and back to Las Cruces, near the scene of the slaying of Garrett. The county has a population of about 6000 and the town a population of 2500.

A CONFEDERATE STATE.

Beyond Las Cruces (the Crosses) is the Organ mountains, rich in minerals. These mountains have been prospected ever since the settlement of the country. This section has no written history before the American occupation, but it is rich in tradition, and was traversed by the Spanish explorers who came up through Mexico en route to what is now Albuquerque and Santa Fe, New Mexico. Mesilla was one of their stopping places. In its earliest settlement by the Americans there were a number of "bad men" who had been driven out of civilization, and they sought refuge in the picturesque Mesilla valley. Early during the Civil War a number of Confederates found their way into the valley with the design of annexing the territory to the Southern Confederacy. The Confederates were operating from Tucson, which was the headquarters of Southern men in the Southwest. Early in 1861 a secession convention was held in "the ancient and honorable pueblo of Tucson," and the Confederate flag, with eleven stars, and bars, was unfurled over the hall. Captain Ewell (afterwards Lieutenant-General in the Confederate Army), was one of the leaders. The plan failed, but in the following July Lieutenant Colonel John R. Baylor, of Texas, with 400 men, captured Fort Fillmore and a garrison of 700 men, and took possession of the Mesilla valley. He organized a state government with himself at its head and raised the Confederate flag. Mesilla was the capital. Thus, New Mexico, or rather part of it, was a state for a moment, and only for a moment.

CHAPTER X.

HISTORY OF BLOODY DEEDS.

Perhaps Lincoln county was the bloodiest spot in the United States from 1875 to 1882, considering its area and population. During that time about two hundred men were killed in southeastern New Mexico, and most of these murders were committed in Lincoln. Lawlessness reigned supreme—the cattle rustlers were in the saddle. Here was the stamping ground of the cattle rustlers and the cattle kings, and for twenty years after the end of the Civil War it was as lawless a section as any in the United States. The Pecos valley caught the first large westbound cattle herds at the time the "maverick" industry was at its worst—that is, stealing unmarked cattle—or, if marked, that did not interfere with the business. It was easier to steal cattle than to raise them. There was a good market at Fort Stanton, where from 1000 to 2000 soldiers were to be fed, and the Mescalero Indian reservation also had to be supplied with beef. Between Fort Stanton (now abandoned), and the Pecos cow herds ran the winding Bonito valley, one of nature's most fertile and beautiful spots. Naturally, it caught bad men, more of these than good men. Many of the cowpunchers were caught with the prevailing cattle-rustler fever, and turned out to be thieves. John Chisholm, a local cattle king, owned about 80,000 head, and many of his punchers became "rustlers" and stole the cattle they were paid to guard. There was a "war" between Chisholm and other cattle kings, and between the Murphy and McSween factions, and it was so revengeful that the United States government troops were called upon to suppress the war.

THE GUN THE ONLY LAW.

The entire country was practically without law—that is, there was law, but it was not enforced, nor were the officers feared or respected. There was, of course, a semblance of law, or its machinery, but men were killed with impunity, and escaped punishment mainly through the fear of the officers to arrest them, or try them when arrested. Most of the executive officers were worthless and lacking in courage. They were failures in everything else, and were elected to these positions because of that worthlessness. The lawless men wanted officers
the United States government troops were called upon to sup-

ally of that type who would sneak round the corner when there was a "gun play," and the sheriff was of that blustering kind who started out after a cattle thief or murderer with a great clatter, and returned without his man. They would take the office because of the salary attached, and, finally, when the desperadoes of the "Billy the Kid" stamp and the cattle rustlers became so powerful that the office was dangerous, it was not wanted. The cheap office seekers stood back, fearing to risk their skin. "Billy the Kid" and his gang were rough-riding the country, and he must be put down, or he would soon become powerful enough to dominate the entire county. A "gun man" was wanted, and one who was not a "bad man." He must be law-abiding, brave and a good shot. During the hottest period of the cattle rustlers' war, in 1879, Patrick F. Garrett, who owned a ranch near Roswell, was offered the position of deputy sheriff. He was known to be brave and a good shot. The thrilling tragedies of those days are as bloody as any recorded in the history of crime. Property was insecure, and the life of every one was in danger—"Billy the Kid" and the "rustlers" defied the officers and lawlessness reigned in Lincoln county. Garrett at once showed his mettle by capturing a number of "bad men" and killing a few others who attempted to get the drop on him. He soon became sheriff, and this was the beginning of the reign of law in Lincoln county.

CHAPTER XI.

THE MAN OF THE HOUR—PAT GARRETT.

In all crises the man for the occasion appears, whether it be a revolution, disaster, political upheaval, or a reign of desperadoes. A man with a steady nerve, strong resolution, quick to act, sure aim, and unquestioned courage, was needed to restore order to this crime-stained district. Garrett was known to possess these qualifications to a marked degree, and he was finally persuaded to accept the office of danger. He was the man of the hour. He did not belong to that class of "bad men" of which so much has been written by scribblers who knew them only by hearsay. He never boasted, but was civil, courteous and peaceable. He soon became one of the best known men in the Southwest, and has a record of accomplishment as a peace officer that is unequaled in the west, and his hands are unstained with innocent blood. He killed only in the discharge of his official duty, and then only when the criminal refused to surrender and in defense of his own life. It was a case of kill or be killed. He never sought nor caused personal trouble. The men he killed were outlaws, and against these he had no malice or personal feelings, other than a public duty. He was always calm, cool, dignified and retiring, and seemed disposed to compromise personal affairs rather than to resort to the "gun." He had a nerve of iron, tempered as steel. That he should meet his death in the manner he did is a cause for much conjecture. He certainly did not expect it at that moment, or would not have been taken unawares. Having "silenced" so many "bad men," he naturally expected the death he had inflicted upon others—he so expressed it as his Fate—but not in the manner it came. In the far west it is the Fate of officers who have been engaged in hunting down and killing criminals in enforcing the law, to die at the hands of criminals or their friends. In the death of Pat Garrett the west has lost one of its best and most fearless old time peace officers. Garrett had enemies—vindictive and malicious. All men of character, especially men of the law, have enemies. He also had many friends—more friends than enemies, who unite with his bereaved family in mouring his death.

There is little need now for "gun men" to serve as officers in the Southwest, and there is not a more peaceful and law-abiding section than Lincoln and Dona Ana counties—the seat of the "cattle rustlers' war," and the territory in which Garrett figured as sheriff, first as sheriff of Lincoln and then of Dona Ana county. To him, more than to any other man, or set of men, the public is indebted for bringing about peace, and exterminating or driving out the "bad gun men." This is a debt which should not be forgotten.

CHAPTER XII.

THE ETHICS OF THE "DROP."

In a country where the revolver was the law, and each man the judge of the necessities of the case, the "drop" was usually the turning point in an affray. It did not, however, always settle an affair, unless the man with the drop was an unerring shot, and had a steady hand. All gun men recognized this, and when they had grievances, real or imaginary, always maneuvered to get his "iron" into position first. The dashing Confederate General, Forrest, always planned to "get there first," and attack the enemy. That was the drop in military tactics. Naturally, this was the method of the early peace officers in the west, for the bad men rarely surrendered without a fight, and several sheriffs were killed before Garrett came upon the scene. Some of them even fought in the face of the drop, as in the case of "Billy the Kid." And some were slow to hold up their hands, relying upon chance to counteract the drop, or, that the officer would not shoot. This was the case of the unknown "man with the red eye."

THE HANGMAN ALSO GOT THE "DROP."

An instance of this kind occurred in Pat Garrett's experience, when he was sheriff of Lincoln county. This thrilling adventure occurred in a saloon on the wind-swept plateau near old Fort Sumner, and near the edge of the Pecos valley. The saloon was kept by a rough looking character who was wanted in the East for murder, and for whose arrest there was a reward of $1200. A description had been sent to Garrett, as it was thought that the assassin may have fled to this isolated strip of country—the rendezvous of outlaws. No one knew the stranger who had recently set up a saloon, and, in those days it was not etiquette to ask questions as to a person's past. Nor were questions answered. The circular described him as having a freckled face and a red spot in one eye. Freckled faced men are common, but the red spot in the eye led Garrett to believe that this was the man wanted. With a deputy they went into the saloon and called for drinks. In relating the affair sometime afterward, Garrett said:

"I told the deputy not to shoot until he saw me go after my gun. I didn't want to hold the man up unless he was the right one; and I wanted to be sure about that identification mark in the eye. When a bartender is waiting on you he will never look you in the face until just as you raise your glass to drink. I told my deputy that we would order a couple of drinks and so get a chance to look this fellow in the eye. I did look him in the eye—and there was the red spot! I dropped my glass and jerked my gun and covered him, but he just wouldn't put up his hands for a while. I didn't want to kill him, but I thought I surely would have to. He kept both of his hands resting on the bar, and I knew he had a gun within three feet of him somewhere. At last he gave in. I treated him well, as I always did a prisoner. We put the irons on him and started for Las Vegas with him in a wagon. The next morning he confessed everything to me. We turned him over and later he was tried and hung. I don't remember his name. I always considered him to be a bad man. So far as the outcome was concerned, he might about as well have gone after his gun."

CHAPTER XIII.

GARRETT'S FIGHT WITH AN OUTLAW.

While sheriff of Dona Ana county, Garrett had a little affair with an outlaw from the Indian Nation, and in this instance the "drop" was not effective. There was a rough and tumble fight, in which the murderer made a desperate struggle and leap for life. In an interview Garrett related the "incident" as follows:

"I was in Las Cruces where there came in a sheriff from the Indian Nation looking for a fugitive who had broke out of a penitentiary after killing a guard and another man or two. This sheriff told me that the criminal in question was the most desperate man he had ever known, and that no matter how we came on him he would put up a fight, and we would have to kill him before we could take him. We located our man, who was cooking on a ranch six or eight miles out of town. I told the sheriff to stay in town, our man would know him and he would not know us. I had a Mexican deputy with me.

DID NOT MIND THE "DROP."

"I put out my deputy on one side of the house and went in. I found my man just wiping his hands on a towel after washing his dishes. I threw down on him and he answered by knocking me with his fist and jumping through the window like a squirrel. I caught at him and tore his shirt off his back, but did not stop him. Then I ran out of the door and caught him on the porch. I did not want to kill him, so I struck him over the head with the handcuffs I had ready for him. He dropped, but came up like a flash and struck me so hard with his fist that I was good and jarred. We fought hammer and tongs for a while, but at length he broke away, sprang through the door, and ran down the hall. He was going to his room after his gun. Just then my Mexican came in, and, having no sentiment about it just whaled away and shot him in the back, killing him on the spot. The doctors said, when they examined the man's body, that he was the most perfect physical specimen they had ever seen. I have forgotten this man's name, too, but I can testify he was a fighter. The sheriff offered me the reward, but I would not take any of it. I told him I would be looking for someone over in his country some day, and was sure he would do as much for me."

CHAPTER XIV.

BONES OF HIS VICTIM AS EVIDENCE.

Another case in which Garrett figured was that of the inhuman brute, Manuel Ribar, alias Eustacio Legada, who murdered another Mexican in 1896 at Mesquite, N. M. The man was killed in the presence of his family, and the assassin then buried the bones of his victim with the pistol he used. He was arrested two years afterward in El Paso by Detective George Harold. Pat Garrett, who was sheriff, took the prisoner back to the scene of his crime, accompanied by Harold. The prisoner confessed the crime and pointed out the spot where his victim was buried and the bones were exhumed. The fellow was taken to Las Cruces and placed in jail. He soon escaped and was at large for eleven years. In March, 1908, a drunken man was arrested in a saloon at El Paso for having a gun in his possession. Detective Harold recognized him as the escaped murderer. He was taken to Las Cruces and placed in jail, and strangely, this was on the day of the funeral of Garrett. As there were no prosecuting witnesses, the man was turned loose, returned to El Paso, and the next day assassinated his cousin, Dolores Legada, and escaped, but was captured next day by Detective Harold.

CHAPTER XV.

THE BLOODY "CATTLE WAR."

Garrett's greatest achievements were while he was sheriff of Lincoln county, which included the destruction of a gang of outlaws under the command of W. H. Bonney, alias "Billy the Kid," and the killing of this famous desperado, whose bloody deeds thrilled the country and gave him the merited name of "fiend." The "Lincoln County War," a strife between cattle men, begun in the Spring of 1876, and continued for several years. Personal feuds were the outgrowth of the "war," and kept the country in terror until Garrett and his deputies finally restored order by dispersing or killing the desperadoes. About this time Bonney and his friends, Jesse Evans and Segura, had returned from a free-booting and Indian fighting expedition in Arizona. They halted at Mesilla and there met James McDaniels, William Morton and Frank Baker, well known cowboys. The cowboys urged Billy and his friends to join them on an excursion to Lincoln county, as there were "hot times on the Pecos." They decided to go, and it was at Mesilla that Wm. H. Bonney was christened "Billy the Kid." McDaniels conferred the nickname upon him, because of his youthful appearance, being only seventeen years of age.

CAUSE OF THE "WAR."

This bloody feud, locally called a war, originated over the question of right to the range, and the illegal branding of cattle—otherwise, the "maverick industry." John Chisholm, the "cattle king of the Pecos," had about 80,000 cattle on the hills and valleys, and claimed a range of nearly 100 miles. He charged that the small proprietors drove his cattle from the range and obliterated his brands with their own. The small owners charged that Chisholm did the same. Thus, there were factions and frequent collisions between their "gun men.

It was not only necessary that a cowboy should be an experienced vaquero, but also a good shot, and one who would fight for his employer. Bonney was a good horseman, an unerring shot, and of reckless daring. The Kid was employed by the Murphy-Donlan faction, which he deserted and joined the John H. Tunstall-McSween faction. In doing his bloody work as a hired gun man, Bonney had killed Morton, Baker and "Billy" Roberts. The sheriff of Lincoln county, Wm. Brady, had a warrant for the arrest of Bonney and his two associates. As Brady and his deputies, George Hindman and J. B. Mathews, were going to the court house in Lincoln, they were fired upon from ambush across the street by "Billy the Kid," Evans and Segura. The sheriff and Hindman were killed and the Kid was slightly wounded by Mathews. The Kid and his gang were now outlawed.

The Kid was now on the road that was soon to cross that of Garrett.

CHAPTER XVI.

ON THE TRACK OF THE KID.

In October, 1880, Sheriff Garrett made his first pursuit of the Kid and his gang. The headquarters of the Kid were at Los Portales, a small cave in a quarry of rock, about fifteen feet high—a rock standing out on a prairie commanding a view of the surrounding country. Near by are two springs. Here the gang concealed their stolen plunder, and had about 100 stolen cattle. A United States detective had informed Sheriff Garrett that W. H. West and Sam Derrick had about $30,000 in counterfeit greenbacks with which they intended buying cattle. Barney Mason was employed to visit the counterfeiters, who were at White Oaks. There he met the Kid, Dave Rudabaugh and Billy Wilson. Mason was suspected and the outlaws escaped. Sheriff Garrett raised a posse of his neighbors near Roswell and started after them. At daylight they sur-
quently rendered me valuable services in my efforts to capture
rounded Derrick's ranch at Bosque Grande, thirty miles from Roswell, and arrested two bad men who had escaped jail, one of whom, Davis, was under a death sentence. At Canaditas they met with Tom O'Fallon, Charlie Bowdre and Tom Pickett, all bad gun men. O'Fallon took twenty-six shots at Garrett (as he afterwards admitted) and Garrett fired three times at him, wounding his horse. It was a long range horse race fight and the outlaws escaped.

CHAPTER XVII.

TWO COWARDLY "BAD MEN."

Next day after this encounter, while Sheriff Garrett was in a store at Puerto de Luna, Juanito Maes, a bully, thief and murderer, approached him, saying, "I hear you have a warrant for me, and I want to surrender." The sheriff replied that he did not have a warrant for him. Then Mariano Leiva, another bully, came up with his hand on his revolver, and made a threat. "I told him to go away, and not bother me," said the sheriff, in relating the affair. "He went out on the porch where he continued in a tirade of abuse against me. He came up with his hand on his revolver, saying that 'No d-- Gringo could arrest him.' I told him that I had no warrant for him, but when I wanted him I would find him. With an oath he raised his left arm in a threatening manner, his hand still on his revolver. I slapped him off the porch. He fired without effect. My pistol went off prematurely, the ball striking at his feet. My second shot went through his shoulder, when he turned and ran, firing as he went, but wide of the mark."

A BRUSH WITH THE GANG.

Shortly after this encounter with the cholos, on the morning of December 18th Sheriff Garrett was out with his deputies in pursuit of the Kid and his gang, who were at Wilcox's ranch, twelve miles east of Fort Sumner. In the meantime the Kid had sent a boy to Fort Sumner. In his sketch of "Billy the Kid" Sheriff Garrett thus writes of the round-up: "Wilcox and his partner, Brazil, were law-abiding, and subsequently rendered me valuable services in my efforts to capture the gang; but, had they been betrayed to the Kid, he would have killed them. Seeing Juan, the spy of the Kid, who was the stepson of Wilcox, I suspected his errand, and after talking to him decided that I could trust him. He told me that the Kid and his gang were coming to Fort Sumner next day in a wagon with a load of beef. Finally, Juan, the spy, promised me that he would deceive the outlaws, and I directed him to write to the Kid that myself and party had gone to Roswell. I then wrote to Wilcox and Brazil that I was at Fort Sumner with thirteen men; that I was on the trail of the gang, and would not stop until I got them or run them out of the country, and asked them to help me. When the spy of the Kid returned with the note the gang laughed at my timidity, and said the news was too good; that they intended to come in after me, and if we had not run away they would have 'shot us up.' Juan, the spy, delivered the other note to Wilcox. I now believed they would come to Fort Sumner and arranged to receive them. There was an old hospital building on the eastern side of the plaza, the direction from which they would come. The wife of Bowdre occupied a room there, and believing that they would visit her, I placed a guard around the building. About 8 o'clock that night they came—two hours before we expected them. Snow was on the ground, increasing the light. In front rade O'Fallon and Pickett. I was under the porch and close against the wall, partly hidden by some harness. When Foliard neared the porch I cried 'Halt!' He reached for his pistol, and Lon Chambers and I both fired. His horse ran. I quickly fired at Pickett, but the flash of Chambers' gun partly blinded me, and my aim was bad, and I missed. O'Fallon wheeled his horse and galloped back, crying, 'Don't shoot, Garrett! I'm killed.' He was uttering cries of mortal agony, and we were convinced that he had received his death wound. I ordered him to throw up his hands, as I would not give him any chance to shoot me, or Mason, his enemy. O'Fallon replied that he could not, as he was dying and begged that we should take him off his horse and let him die easily. Holding our guns down on him we lifted him off, took his gun out of the scabbard, and took off his pistol, which was full cocked, and then carried him into the house. He begged me to kill him, saying that if I was his friend I would put him out of his misery. I told him that I was not a friend of his kind, who sought to murder me because I was doing my duty. He told who was with him and died within an hour. Pickett was unhurt, but almost scared to death. He ran his horse down and reached Wilcox's ranch on foot and hid in a hay stack until his companions, the Kid, Rudabaugh, Bowdre and Wilson, came along. It must have been amusing to witness that fellow's change from cowardice to bravado when he was out of danger. He swaggered about, saying: 'Boys, I got that d— long-legged fellow that cried 'Halt!' I had my gun on my saddle and poured it into him. I got him, sure!'

SPYING OUT THE SITUATION.

During our encounter with O'Fallon and Pickett, the posse fired upon the Kid and the others, only killing Rudabaugh's horse. The gang was now reduced to five. They stayed at Wilcox's ranch that night, throwing out pickets, and sent Brazil to Fort Sumner next day to spy out the land. They had suspected Wilcox and Brazil of betraying them, but had been reassured by them.

As the gang were riding toward the hospital building the Kid was in front of O'Fallon, but with all his daring, he was also very cautious. Under the pretext of wanting tobacco, he rode back to one of his men, otherwise he would have caught the bullets O'Fallon received. Perhaps it was a lucky presentiment that often guides one to his Fate.

CHAPTER XVIII.

CAPTURE OF THE KID AND HIS GANG.

On the next day Brazil arrived at Fort Sumner and reported to Garrett that the Kid had asked him to come and find out the situation. Garrett told him to report that he had with him only Mason and three Mexicans, that he was scared, and was going back to Roswell, and to remain at his ranch if the gang were there; otherwise, to return. "The faithful friend," wrote Garrett, "returned about 12 that night; it was very cold and his beard was full of icicles. He reported that the Kid and his four companions had taken supper at Wilcox's ranch, and then left. We got on their trail and found them at a deserted house built by Alejandro Perea. We surrounded the house. There were three horses tied to the projecting rafters, and as there were five men, two horses were evidently in the house. There was no door, only an opening where a door had been. Shivering with cold we waited until daylight. I had a good description of the Kid's dress, especially his hat. I told the possee that it was my intention to kill the Kid, and the others would surrender, as the Kid had said he would never surrender, and I believed he would die fighting. My position commanded the doorway, and I told the men that when I brought up my gun, to all raise and fire.

THE KID APPEARS.

About daylight, continued the sheriff, a man answering to the description of the Kid, appeared in the doorway. I threw my gun to my shoulder and there were seven reports. Charley Bowdre reeled and fell back into the house. Wilson, one of the gang, called out that Bowdre was shot and wanted to come out. I told him to come out with his hands up. As Bowdre started out, the Kid drew Bowdre's revolver in front of him and asked him if he did not want revenge before he died. Bowdre came out with his hands up. He recognized me, and came straight towards the house, streaming with blood. He said: "I wish—I wish—" and then, in a whisper, "I am dying!" I laid him on my blankets and he died instantly. I saw a movement of the ropes of the horses, and suspected that the bandits were attempting to lead the horses inside. I shot a horse and it fell in the doorway, barricading it. To prevent another attempt I shot the ropes in two which held the other two horses and they walked away.

I opened a conversation with the besieged, said the sheriff, and the Kid was their spokesman. I asked them how they were fixed in there.

"Pretty well," replied the Kid. "But we have no wood to get breakfast."

"Come out and get some, and be a little sociable!"

"Can't do it, Pat. Business is too confining. No time to run around."

"Didn't you fellows forget part of your program yesterday? You were to come in on us at Fort Sumner, give us a square fight, set us afoot, and drive us down the Pecos." My banter caused the Kid to understand that he had been betrayed and he became reticent.

We sent back for provisions, as we thought the siege would last some time. About 4 o'clock we began cooking dinner. The odor of roasting meat was too much for the half-starved gang, and Rudabaugh stuck out from the window a kerchief that had once been white, saying they would surrender if guaranteed against violence. This I promised, and told them to come out with their hands up. The Kid, Rudabaugh, Wilson and Pickett came out, were given their supper, when we put the irons on them and started for Las Vegas. The Kid told me that their plan was to get the horses in the house and attempt to get away. We finally reached Las Vegas, our objective point being Santa Fe, as there were United States warrants against all except Pickett.

CHAPTER XIX.

A BLUSTERING MOB AT LAS VEGAS.

There has been considerable fiction written about the Kid, his deeds, and his "seraglio" where he lived in splendor, surrounded by his female favorites. A cheap Eastern magazine has given a hair-lifting account of the manner in which the Kid aided Sheriff Garrett in standing off a mob, the sheriff having loaned his handcuffed prisoner one of his six-shooters. Sheriff Garrett, in his "Life of Billy the Kid," gives a different account of the affair, and as he was present, and the yellow magazinist was not, Mr. Garrett's statement should be considered as the truthful one. He writes:

"On the morning of December 27th we took the Kid, Rudabaugh and Wilson from the prison at Vegas and got on the cars to take them to Santa Fe. Deputies Stewart and Mason were my deputies. We soon noticed a crowd of Mexicans armed with revolvers. Their object was to take Rudabaugh off the train. The authorities there had previously attempted to hold him, as he had killed a jailer at that place. But I told them that he was a United States prisoner, and that as I was also a United States deputy marshal, I would take him to Santa Fe. I asked Stewart if we should fight the mob, and he replied, 'Yes; let's make a good one.' Their object was to mob Rudabaugh. We were pledged to protect him. Stewart guarded one door of the coach and I the other. These armed ruffians crowded about the car, but none of them stated their business, or demanded Rudabaugh. Deputy Sheriff Romero headed a mob of five and approached the platform where I was standing, flourishing their revolvers. 'Let's go right in and take him out!' one of them exclaimed, and they pushed their deputy up on the platform, crowding after him. I merely requested them, mildly, to get down, and they slid to the ground like a covey of hardback turtles off the banks of the Pecos.

THE KID WANTS TO FIGHT.

"Rudabaugh was excited, but the Kid and Wilson seemed unconcerned. I told them not to be uneasy; that we would fight if the mob entered the car, and that I would arm them and let them take a hand. The Kid's eyes glistened, as he said, 'All right, Pat. All I want is a six-shooter. There is no danger, though; these fellows won't fight.'

"True enough, the mob weakened. All they wanted was for some one to coax them to desist, so that it would not look like a square back down. I placed the prisoners safely in the Santa Fe jail.

"In a few days the desperadoes became active. They attempted to escape by digging a hole through the adobe walls and hiding the dirt under their bedding. The scheme failed. Rudabaugh was convicted of robbing the United States mail, but no sentence was passed, and on the demand of the territorial authorities he was tried for the murder of the jailer at Las Vegas and sentenced to be hanged. He escaped from jail. Billy Wilson, who. with the Kid. killed James Carlyle, was convicted at Mesilla."

CHAPTER XX.

THE KID IS SENTENCED TO BE HANGED.

Billy the Kid was also taken to Mesilla, where he was tried in March, 1881, for the murder of Roberts at the Mescalero Apache agency, three years previous. He was acquitted, but was immediately tried on the charge of assassinating William Brady, sheriff of Lincoln county, in March, 1878. He was sentenced to be hanged at Lincoln on the 13th day of May, 1881. He was taken from Mesilla by Deputy Marshal Robert Ollinger and Deputy Sheriff David Woods of Dona Ana county, and turned over to Sheriff Garrett at Fort Stanton, nine miles west of the town of Lincoln. Lincoln county had no jail and a dilapidated two-story store building was used as the county building. The Kid was placed in a room in the second story, hand-cuffed, with Deputy Sheriff J. W. Bell and Deputy Marshal Robert Ollinger as guards.

THE KID HAS NO TASTE FOR THE ROPE.

One week after his arrival the Kid escaped, killing his two guards. It was a most daring deed, cunningly planned and brutal in its execution. The Kid was the only living witness of his escape, and his story is substantially as follows: At his own request, Bell accompanied the Kid down stairs, and as they returned Bell permitted the Kid to walk some distance ahead. As the Kid turned on the landing of the stairs he was hidden from Bell. He threw himself against the door of the armory, seized a six-shooter, and as Bell advanced at the head of the stairs, fired upon him at a distance of about twelve feet. Bell ran out and fell dead. The Kid then slipped his handcuffs, threw them at the body, saying, "Here, d— you, take these, too!" He then ran to the sheriff's office and got a double-barreled shotgun belonging to Ollinger. Hearing the shot, Ollinger had started across the street. Seeing him, the Kid shouted from above, "Hello, Bob!" and as Ollinger looked up, the Kid fired, killing him instantly. He fired the other barrel into the prostrate form. Then, breaking the gun across the railing, he threw the pieces at the corpse, with the same remark when he threw his handcuffs at his first victim. He then armed himself with a Winchester and two revolvers. He hailed an old man and made him bring him a file, with which he filed the shackels from one leg, and then held up a man for a horse belonging to Billy Burt, clerk of the court. The horse broke loose twice from the man and in about an hour the Kid mounted, and with the shackels dangling to his leg, rode toward Las Tablas.

There was a sad fatality in Ollinger's case. That morning he loaded his shotgun in the presence of the Kid, placing eighteen buck shot in each barrel, and remarked, "The man who gets this will feel it." Within a few hours he was literally riddled with thirty-six shot at the hands of the Kid.

Sheriff Garrett was at White Oaks at the time of the sad tragedy, but before leaving, he especially charged his deputies to be very vigilant, as the Kid was tricky, daring, and would at the slightest chance fight desperately for his life, especially as the gallows loomed up before him. His advice was disregarded and the outlaw escaped, adding two murders to his bloody record.

CHAPTER XXI.

WANDERINGS OF THE OUTLAW.

Billy the Kid was next heard of at Las Tablas, where he had stolen a horse from Andy Richardson. He rode the animal to within a few miles of Fort Sumner, when it broke loose and Billy walked into town. Here he stole a horse from Montgomery Bell, which he rode away bareback. For some time he stayed with a sheep herder on Pete Maxwell's ranch, 35 miles east of Fort Sumner. He was continually on the move from sheep herder's camps to Canaditas, Arenoso, and Fort Sumner. This fugitive life lasted about two and a half months—hovering around the scenes of his crimes of the past two years. There seems to be a fascination, or an impelling power, which directs a criminal to the scenes of his crimes, notwithstanding the danger. He was an outlaw, under sentence of death, and yet he lingered under the shadow of the gallows. He had many friends, and others aided him through fear.

ON THE TRAIL OF THE KID.

Upon being informed of the tragedy, Sheriff Garrett hastened back, and with deputies Tip. McKinney and Joe Poe, took up the trail of the Kid, which led to his death. Garrett had learned of Billy's movements, and he was expected to visit the house of Pete Maxwell. The house has long since been torn down, and on the site is only a rough quadrangle of crumbling earthen walls. In writing of this last scene in the tragic life of the most famous desperado of the southwest, Mr. Garrett describes how the Kid was killed:

THE SHERIFF GOT THE DROP ON HIM.

"Pete Maxwell's bed was in this corner of the room, and I was sitting in the dark and talking to Pete, who was in bed. The Kid passed John Poe and Tip. McKinney, my deputies, right over there on what was then the gallery, and came through the door right here. He could not tell who I was. 'Pete,' he whispered, who is it?' He had his pistol, a double action .41, in his hand, and he motioned toward me with it as he spoke, still not recognizing me. That was about all there was to it. I supposed he would shoot me, and I leaned over to the left so that he would hit me in the right side and not kill me so dead but what I could kill him, too. I was just a shade too quick for him. His pistol went off as he fell, but I don't suppose he ever knew who killed him or how he was killed."

CHAPTER XXII.

WILLIAM H. BONNEY, ALIAS "BILLY THE KID."

William H. Bonney, whose daring deeds and brutal crimes gained for him an infamous record equaled by no other desperado in the southwest, was born in the city of New York on November 23rd, 1859. At the time of his tragic death he was in his 22nd year, and had killed twenty-seven men—perhaps more. In 1862 the Bonney family, consisting of the father, mother and two boys, of whom Billy was the eldest, emigrated to Coffeyville, Kansas. The father died soon after and the widow with her two boys removed to Colorado, where she married ——— Antrim. They then removed to Georgetown, New Mexico, and then to Santa Fe. Billy was then about five years of age. At this tender age he began to show his viciousness among his companions—his inherent criminal nature was asserting its mastery, and developing him for a career of crime. In about three years the family again moved and located at Silver City, New Mexico. Here Billy learned to play cards, and gradually drifted into the vices of the day, except that of drinking. He became an expert poker player and monte dealer, and this at the early age of 12 years. He attended the public school, and, though he was of average intelligence, learned but little—his ambition was to become a "bad man." It was in his nature, and he could not overcome it, had he desired. Even then he was bold and daring, and, at times he was frank and generous. His real nature was ever masked by a smile, which, at times, was sardonic or fiendish, revealing a trait he wished to conceal.

HIS UNHAPPY HOME.

Billy's mother, Kathleen, was of Irish descent. She was about medium height, straight in form, with regular features, light blue eyes and reddish hair. She kept a boarding house, and so far as known, had a good reputation. Billy loved his mother, about the only human being for whom he cared. His step-father, Antrim, treated him cruelly. In about four years, or in 1871, the cruelty of his step-father drove him from home, and from his mother's influence. He attributed this as the cause of his criminal career, and while on the "war path" expressed his desire to meet that step-father just for one minute. His mother soon died, and Billy now had no family ties, and his career of blood began.

HIS FIRST FIGHT.

Billy's first personal difficulty, and which led to his first killing, was in defense of his mother's name. In passing a group of idlers, one of the cowards made an insulting remark about her. Billy overheard it and with burning anger, struck the cur in the mouth and then reached for a rock. The brute made a rush toward Billy, and was knocked down by Ed. Moulton. Billy got a rifle and was about to "throw down" on the fellow, when he was restrained by Moulton. Moulton and Billy became friends, because of this act of friendship in punishing the bully.

BILLY KILLS HIS FRIEND'S ANTAGONIST.

About three weeks afterwards, Ed. Moulton got into trouble. While striving against two "shoulder strikers," the bully whom he had knocked down for insulting Billy's mother appeared upon the scene and sought revenge on Moulton, rushing upon him with a heavy bar-room chair. The coward took this opportunity, there now being three against one. Billy was usually on hand when there was anything stirring, either as a principal or a spectator, and seeing his friend Moulton assaulted by three, drew his knife and stabbed the insulter of his mother before he could strike Moulton. The fellow fell dead at his feet. Bonney then fled from Silver City, an outlaw. He wandered three days and nights without seeing any one except a sheep herder, who supplied him with food. He was on foot, making his way to Arizona. At Knight's ranch he stole a horse—his first theft. He had now entered upon his career of crime.

CHAPTER XXIII.

BILLY MAKES HIS FIRST RAID.

In about three weeks he arrived at Fort Bowie, with a companion, whom Billey called "Alias,"—the only name the fellow gave. Both rode one horse. Here they sold the horse, borrowed an old rifle and a pistol from soldiers, and started out on their first raid, on foot. The Chiracahua Apaches, on the reservation near by, were peaceable, and there was no danger in visiting them. Billy spoke Spanish, and so did some of the Indians. The object of the youthful bandits was to get two horses. They met three Indians who refused to sell their ponies. In describing the affair to Sheriff Garrett, a few years afterward, Billy said, in a matter of fact way: "It was a ground hog case; here were three savages revelling in luxury and refusing aid to two free-born white Americans, foot-sore and hungry. They had twelve good ponies, a supply of blankets, and five pony loads of pelts. The plunder had to change hands, and as one live Indian could put a hundred United States soldiers on our trail in two hours, and as a dead Indian could not, there was no alternative. In three minutes there were three dead Indians lying around, and with the ponies and plunder we skipped. There was no fight—it was the softest thing I ever struck."

"LIVING THE PACE."

The youthful bandits sold their plunder to immigrants from Texas on the road about 100 miles from Fort Bowie. They returned to the fort splendidly mounted and armed, and with a large amount of money. Naturally, they soon became on good terms with government officials and citizens of Fort Bowie, San Carlos, Apache Pass, San Simon and the surrounding settlements, as they spent money lavishly. The military authorities made no inquiries as to the murder and robbery of the Indians, whom they were sent there to protect; and.

as no money could be made by prosecuting the criminals, the civil authorities took no notice of the crime.

The bandits next went to Tucson, where Billy's skill as a monte dealer came into play, and enabled them to lead a gay life among the Amazons of the old pueblo.

CHAPTER XXIV.

A "BUNCO" HORSE RACE.

The pleasures of the fandango and life in the pueblo became monotonous to the young bandits, and they again started upon the road. Meeting a band of ten Indians near San Simon they proposed a horse race. Billy was riding a fine animal, but put his bets on an inferior one, which was ridden by his companion "Alias." The Indians, naturally thinking that Billy was not far removed from a fool, placed their money, of course upon their best pony. Billy said that he would ride his friend's horse, but insisted that his friend should hold the stakes. Naturally distrustful of the pale face, the Indians did not suspect a trick, and insist that somebody should hold the man who held the stakes. At the word, three horses passed under the bar, instead of two. The extra horse carried Billy's friend with the stakes, and he distanced the other two, not stopping for several miles.

There was a "big talk" between the Kid and the Indians and they came near scalping Billy, but he seemed to be innocent of any job, and charged that his wicked partner had acted in bad faith, and argued that he was the greatest loser, as the fellow had his horse, and also the money he had bet. He had not only lost these, but also his confidence in his friend and in humanity generally. The Indians grunted their sympathy for Billy and he rode away to meet his friend "Alias" next day and divide the money.

BILLY MAKES HIS SECOND KILLING.

Shortly afterwards, Billy had a quarrel with a soldier at Fort Bowie and killed him. Billy was always reticent as to this affair, only saying that the fellow was a bully, and had refused to pay money lost at cards. It was believed that there was a woman in the case. During the quarrel the fellow, who was much larger than Billy, attempted to whip him, but the Kid got the drop. He then fled to Sonora and without his former companion "Alias."

CHAPTER XXV.

BILLY MAKES ANOTHER KILLING.

Arriving at Guaymas, Billy at once plunged into a career of gaming. His skill as a monte dealer and knowledge of Spanish established him among the Mexicans, and he soon became a successful gambler. He formed a partnership with Melquiades Segura, who later accompanied Billy across the border to New Mexico. They frequented the gaming house of "Don" Jose Martinez, a monte dealer, who was envious of Bonney, and, like all bullies, made insulting remarks when he saw that Billy did not desire a difficulty. Whenever Bonney entered the place Martinez began a tirade of abuse against "Gringos," having first placed his revolver on the table in front of him. The insults were directed at Bonney. He decided to settle the affair —and the bully.

About 9 o'clock one night, he and Segura saddled their horses, and prepared for their departure. The horses were left in charge of Segura a short distance from the gambling house. Billy entered alone. As soon as he neared the table, Martinez placed his revolver upon the table, and began his insulting remarks, as was expected. Billy's pistol was in the scabbard. Before putting his hand on his revolver, Billy said to the bully: "Jose, do you fight as bravely with that pistol at your hand as you do with your mouth?" And then Billy's hand fell upon the butt of his own pistol. Martinez counted too much on his advantage, as he had his pistol on the table, almost in his hand, while Billy's was still in the scabbard. But, with that rapidity for which he was noted, Bonney drew his weapon at the first move of the hand of Martinez, and shot the fellow through the head, killing him instantly. Billy slapped his hand to his right ear—the bullet of his antagonist had just grazed it.

THE FLIGHT AND PURSUIT.

In a moment Bonney and his friend Segura were on their horses, headed for the mountains of Chihuahua. About twenty Mexicans started in pursuit, which they continued for ten days. They only found the jaded horses of the desperadoes, who had exchanged them for fresh ones. A large reward was offered by the family of Martinez, and several attempts were made to trap Bonney and Segura into returning to that country, but they did not like the climate.

CHAPTER XXVI.

BAD LUCK, BUT BROKE A MONTE GAME.

Bonney and Segura made their way to the city of Chihuahua where their usual good luck at monte failed them. Fortune, like woman, is fickle, and there are times when it smiles, and when it frowns. Bonney's skill at dealing monte, and his nonchalant, dashing style, excited the envy of the other gamblers, and, like those outcasts, they became his enemies, merely because he was their superior in the "black art." The trouble soon came, and the envious gamblers lost. One night Bonney won a large amount at a monte table, when the dealer closed the bank, and sneeringly remarked that he did not have enough money to pay him, while at the moment he had raked more than enough doubloons into his leather sack to pay Billy. The dealer leered at Bonney, as he left the table with his well filled sack. Bonney and Segura made no reply, and left the house.

THE MEXICAN MONTE DEALER DISAPPEARED.

That monte dealer did not reach home that night with his sack of doubloons. He disappeared mysteriously, and so did the gold. Billy and Segura went into seclusion for several days and on the following few nights three other monte dealers were held up as they were returning home with their "banks." Each of these men had offended either Bonney or Segura.

Billy and his companion now decided that the atmosphere of Chihuahua was not congenial, and they left for New Mexico. They settled their bills along the route in Spanish gold, from a buckskin sack, prettily wrought in gold and silver thread lace. Billy was always reticent about this affair of the monte dealer who refused to pay him, and even his friends did not press their questions.

CHAPTER XXVI.

NOT OF THE "YELLOW KID" TYPE.

William H. Bonney, better known as "Billy the Kid," was not the typical character depicted by yellow-kid magazine and newspaper writers. He was about the last person one would select for a "gun man." He was never "attired" as a brigand or guerrilla. He usually wore a black frock coat, dark pantaloons, and vest, a neat boot, and a wide hat to protect his face from the sun. He swore, naturally, but his oaths were not of the obscene kind—he expressed them in better phraseology, bordering on the picturesque—if swearing can be picturesque. He was not beastly in his demeanor, not so much as some of the "society" men of today. He was polite and cordial, inviting confidence. It was one of his traits, and a very rare one, to never betray a friend. He was about five feet and eight inches in stature, stood straight, and weighed about 135 pounds. His form was well knit, and he was very muscular, tough and light and active. His hair was of a dark brown, glossy and luxuriant, and not worn long as depicted by "fake" magazinists. His eyes were a deep blue, dotted with spots of hazel hue, and were bright and expressive. His face was oval, the most noticeable feature being two projecting upper front teeth, which was not a disfigurement, but sufficiently prominent to attract attention. Newspaper fakers have described these as "fangs" and depicted him as an ogre. He was handsomer than the majority of men.

CHAPTER XXVII.

THE LAST SCENE OF ALL.

The life of Wm. H. Bonney practically began with a romance and a death, and it so ended, with the difference that in the last he was the one killed. It is believed that the soldier whom he killed at Fort Bowie had attacked him because of his jealousy—he suspected his wife and Billy.

On the evening that he came to Maxwell's ranch house, and his death, it was to meet his lady love. But his blissful anticipations were shattered by a bullet. He was buried near the ranch house by the side of his former companions in crime, Bowdre and O'Fallon. Time and the elements have obliterated all trace of the graves, and he is only remembered by his many bloody deeds. He was one of the most picturesque criminals in the bloody annals of the southwest, and he wrote his infamous history in the blood of his victims.

CHAPTER XXVIII.

PEACE AND PROSPERITY NOW REIGN IN LINCOLN.

Law and order now reign—the bad gun men have been silenced, or forced to leave the country, and "cattle rustlers" have ceased from troubling stock men. This picturesque section, once the most disorderly, perhaps, of any in the far west, is now one of the most peaceful and prosperous. It is estimated that about 200 men were killed in "bloody Lincoln county" from its earliest settlement to the time that Sheriff Garrett stampeded the Kid's band, and put a quietus upon the leader. With the restoration of order, settlers began to come in, and then the railroad came, and the rush for farming and grazing lands continued, and still continues.

Lincoln county is one of the best cattle sections in New Mexico. In 1883, it headed the list, containing about 100,000 head, and was ranked as sixth in sheep, containing 137,000 head. Naturally, the "rustlers" found this an inviting field. The country is watered by the Rio Pecos, (formerly the Rio de Las Vacas, or cows), and its branches. One of its branches is Rio Bonito, which courses through a fine grazing section, and which has given its name to a thriving town, Bonito, which is in the heart of a good agricultural and mining section.

Lincoln county occupies the southeastern corner of the territory of New Mexico, and has an area of about 20,000 square miles. The territory was taken from Socorro and created as a county in 1869. It then had a population of about 2000. The county seat was located at Rio Bonito (formerly Las Placitas), and was then changed to Lincoln, its present name. Of its area, 5,483,000 acres, the largest part is agricultural, and all of it well watered by rivers and numerous smaller streams, which are fed by mountain springs. The mountains are heavily timbered and about 500,000,000 feet of standing timber is found in the immediate vicinity of Bonito. Rich mines are also being developed in the Bonito mining district, which promise to place the town of Bonito, once the haunt of bandit and cutthroat, alongside of Cripple Creek and Goldfields.

In the Sierra Blanca are large deposits of pure graphite, also, salt and coal. There are other mining districts at Jicarilla, White Oaks, Vera Cruz, Nogal and Capitan.

THE END.

El Capitan Mountain, near the Prosperous Town of Bonito.

A Forest Reserve Ranger on one of the Bonito Timber Slopes

The Bonito River

In the House in the lower left hand corner of this picture Mart. Nelson, a desperado and cattle thief, killed an entire family and was himself shot to death by officers in the year of 1880

FILTER PRESS
Wild And Woolly West BOOKS

Phone 303 481-2523

1.	Choda	Thirty Pound Rails, 1956.
2.	Clemens	Celebrated Jumping Frog, 1965.
3.	Banks	Uncle Jim's Book of Pancakes, 1967.
4.	Service	Yukon Poems, 1967.
5.	Cushing	My Adventures in Zuni, 1967.
6.	Englert	Oliver Perry Wiggins, 1968. *(Out of Print)*
7.	Matthews	Navajo Weavers & Navajo Silversmiths, 1968.
8.	Campbell,	Wet Plates & Dry Gulches, 1970.
9.	Banks	Alferd Packer's Wilderness Cookbook, 1969.
10.	Faulk	Simple Methods of Mining Gold, 1969.
11.	Rusho	Powell's Canyon Voyage, 1969.
12.	Hinckley	Transcontinental Rails, 1969.
13.	Young	The Grand Canyon, 1969.
14.	Gehm	Nevada's Yesterdays, 1970.
15.	Seig	Tobacco, Peace Pipes, & Indians, 1971.
16.	Conrotto	Game Cookery Recipes, 1971.
17.	Scanland	Life of Pat. F. Garrett, 1971.
18.	Hunt	High Country Ghost Town Poems, 1962.
19.	Arpad	Buffalo Bill's Wild West, 1971.
20.	Wheeler	Deadwood Dick's Leadville Lay, 1971.
21.	Powell	The Hopi Villages, 1972.
22.	Bathke	The West in Postage Stamps, 1973.
23.	Hesse	Southwestern Indian Recipe Book, 1973.
24.	Vangen	Indian Weapons, 1972.
25.	MacDonald	Cockeyed Charley Parkhurst, 1973.
26.	Schwatka	Among the Apaches, 1974.
27.	Bourke Remington	General Crook in the Indian Country, *and* A Scout With the Buffalo Soldiers, 1974.
28.	Powell	An Overland Trip to the Grand Canyon, 1974.
29.	Harte	Luck of Roaring Camp & other sketches, 1975
30.	Remington	On the Apache Indian Res. & Among the Cheyennes, 1974
31.	Ferrin	Many Moons Ago, 1976.
32.	Kirby	Saga of Butch Cassidy, 1977
33.	Isom	Fox Grapes, 1977

PRINTED IN THE UNITED STATES OF AMERICA

½

901 902 903 904 905 906 907 908 909 910 911 912